Teshelle Combs

This
One
Has
Pockets

Teshelle Combs Books

Copyright © 2020 by Teshelle Combs

All Rights reserved, including the rights of reproduction in print or online in any whole or partial form.

Manufactured in the United States of America.

Book layout and design by Nate Combs Media.

ISBN-13: 979-8612779605

For those who feel you have to lie
about sad nights and long days.
I see you.

Teshelle Combs

This
One
Has
Pockets

1

The start is when my door closes.

The reluctant click of the lock falling into place.

I wait until the smudges leave the brass door knob—

A slow fade.

This, I do every time.

I let the moon creep up a little more.

I wonder if it's nervous, facing the world.

I would be nervous.

I'm nervous now.

When things end,

When doors close,

The next phase begins.

Who knows the revelries

Taking place on the

Dark side of my moon?

2

Hands and knees
Are what it takes
To make it to
My crawl space.

I fold in my legs
And peel up the carpet's edge.

Paper bound with paper.

I hold the notebook in my gritty fingers.
I'm sandpaper compared to its smooth finish.

No lines on its pages.
The lines are elsewhere…black marks cast by window blinds
And furniture pushed against the white wall.

My space.
My book.
Mine.

3

I don't need a pen.
I don't need a pencil.
I put the book on my knees
And my forehead on the book.

Each tear is special.

People don't tell you that
Sort of thing.
In fact, we spend no time
Teaching on tears.

When I'm through,
If I look hard enough,
I can see where the tears
Changed things.
Warped the paper
And made their dark marks.

4

If anyone was listening,

They would hear the sound

Of the drops.

Their own arhythmic symphony.

An atonal refrain.

No one is listening.

I am listening.

Long after I close the book,

And crawl out of my space,

I hear the pitter-patter of

The song.

Not in my head, no.

Following me.

5

My shadow is composed of sounds.

Pitter-patter. Drip drop.

It clings to my heels.

The whispers grate themselves on the concrete.

I hear them gasp with relief when I stop moving.

But I move more often than not.

It is nice to hear

something.

6

The ceiling is open
At the shop I frequent.
A veil peeled back—
The sky like a bride revealed.

I wait at a round table,
The edge cutting into my elbows.
I am crying, of course.
Dripping and dropping.

No one notices.
They sip and tip and leave.
Until the boy.
The boy who notices.

Across the shop,
He stares.
Shadow eyes.
He hears. He sees.

7

In some moments,

The physics of space changes...

When two bodies

Move closer together.

The boy.

The boy who notices.

He spins over to me

And sits in a metal chair.

He orders a coffee

And puts his forehead to mine.

It is a mistake, the next part.

The posture, you see...

My tears slip into his cup.

8

The boy.

The boy who notices.

He does not ask me about my shadow.

He only taps his fingers to the song.

He only hums the chorus.

He touches my hand.

How polished, how smooth he is.

I wonder

If he is nervous.

9

Up he gets.

One foot first, as if to test it out.

Then the other.

Tentative.

He slides into the coffee cup.

I peer over the rim.

Ripples.

No one notices

The boy who notices.

I am nervous.

I do not see even the outline of him in there.

Only brown

And sloshing.

10

I take the cup

From the table.

I ask my shadow

To quiet just enough

For me to think.

But it does not hear me

Or does not care.

It is louder,

Like fingernails against asphalt.

I take the cup with the boy who notices

And remind myself not to take a sip.

11

Reluctant click.

Hands and knees.

I pull the cup in after me.

Sweat on my brow this time.

I have never brought anyone

To my space.

No one has ever

Seen my book.

I set the boy in the cup

Down on my pages.

He leaves a ring of brown.

I want to pick him up,

But there are rings

Everywhere.

And the pages warp.

Brown.

I cry.

It does not matter

Where my tears fall

This time.

12

Book under the carpet and

Cup on the sill

So the boy can see

The moon change.

I tuck my hands in my pockets

And pull out fistfuls

Of coffee.

I do not panic.

I stir him a little

In his cup

And hope he

Likes the swish of light.

13

I lose a sleep,

Standing by the boy

In his cup

On the sill

Under the moon.

My fingers are sticky from

Pretending my pockets

Are not filled with

Him.

But now

I hear

Sloshing and swishing

With the deep breathing

Of my long shadow.

14

I do things.

Work things. Home things.

There is dripping on the carpet

And the sidewalks.

From the tips of my hair.

Brown.

And each drop is a whisper

Of a song.

I leave the boy in a trail behind me.

15

I find myself lucky.

He talks to me.

I don't know what he says,

But the whispers tickle the back of my neck.

So nice to have company.

Perhaps he is composing

A new song.

He drips down my collarbone

And trickles over my spine.

No one notices.

16

I was worried

The boy

And my shadow

Would argue,

Would fight.

But there became

No contest.

They were the same.

I wanted to be the same,

But shadows need

People to follow

And places to slink.

17

Dinner time.

When people obligated

By biology eat things

Together alone.

I leave puddles

On the table

Underneath the salt and pepper shakers.

The people who don't notice me,

They make noise with their mouths.

They scream, maybe. Chew.

They throw glass, maybe.

It is hard for me to tell.

They are all crying

But they can't tell, either.

I am happy the boy is with me.

18

The outline of me

Is hard to make out.

I waver.

Each step leaves pools

Until I am unsure

Whether I leave the puddles

Or bocome them.

I make it through

To the setting of the sun.

One of those when the moon is up before

The day is finished.

It is so nervous.

I am less nervous.

19

Lock.

Crawl.

Cup.

Book.

Tears.

Brown.

Moon.

Whisper.

Slosh.

20

My favorite spot.

The ceiling peels back

So the clouds can witness

The procession.

Me alone.

Everyone alone.

My shadow takes a breather

Beneath my chair.

21

At the shop,

There is a boy.

The boy.

The boy who notices.

He stares with shadow eyes.

He stomps over

And sits in a metallic chair

Across from me.

He has something for me.

A rose.

For me. For me.

There are some moments

When time shifts

To make space

For me. For me.

22

The boy.

The boy who notices.

He touches the pool of me

And I let him touch me.

He sighs

And lies down in

One of the petals.

White wraps around him

And he closes his eyes.

How neatly his edges curl.

How smooth and silken when I touch them

With sandpaper hands.

23

Yes. Yes.

I put him in my pocket.

Squeeze him in my palms.

I do not mean to bruise him,

But he is so gentle.

The petals stick to the coffee

On my hands—

A fragrant whisper.

24

Petals and puddles.

At the grocery store,

With the list my mother

Nailed to my door.

I drag my feet

Through the aisles.

The petals are like stones

In my pockets.

I am nervous.

Drowning in my own self

Will mean

I did not bring home

The right cereal.

There will be screaming.

I drag. I drag. Yes. Yes.

No one notices.

25

Someone is asking for money

At the conveyor belt.

I hand them white petals

Soaked in brown.

The someone wrinkles their nose

And wipes their hands on their apron.

They want to know if I am alright,

But it comes out in screaming.

I am used to hearing whispers.

And so I take the right cereal

And leave the change.

26

Reluctant.

I press him

Into my book.

27

I bring him to dinner with me.

Instead of eating, I sprinkle him

On my empty plate.

I crush petals between my teeth.

He tastes like coffee.

Instead of screaming,

I let the brown leak from my ears.

How nice to have company.

28

My shadow

Is becoming

Too heavy.

Too much.

I am bearing

Him.

But barely.

Once, I try to

Unhinge him

From my ankles.

I cannot.

My hands become

Moon beams.

My ankles become

stems.

29

I lose a sleep.

I am losing all the sleeps.

My shadow tugs me out of bed.

I stumble across the sidewalks,

Grating against the concrete.

We are taking a long walk

To the beach.

The whole way is rose petals

And the sea is brown.

I lie down in the salt and pepper sand

And he lets me.

30

Under the moon,

The ceiling peeled back,

After a time,

A bee stings my cheek.

I am overjoyed.

At last, a change.

I thank him

For the company.

It feels good

To be noticed.

31

The boy.

The boy who notices.

Finds me on the corner,

Sleeping on the curb.

He brushes the sand from my coffee hair.

He rubs rose oil on the stinger in my cheek.

He finds me.

He finds me on all the corners.

32

The boy whispers.

I am not sure

But I will help him.

He has burying to do.

I can be so good at burying.

I can be so good at being.

I can be so good.

33

My shadow lifts me

Onto the back of a bee.

He holds me steady

And lets me sleep

With my head against the

Rim of a cup.

I wonder if he is nervous

Flying so close to the moon.

I am nervous,

But only a little.

34

We eat white rose petals

In the empty lot

Behind the grocery store

Against the dumpster.

Then we start digging.

I was right.

I am good.

I don't ask who we bury.

The music is too loud

For me to hear

Anything but whispers

And screams.

And sloshing.

35

I make it back home

With dirt in my pockets.

Clumps of mud in my hands when I

Stuff them in.

I cannot stay still long.

He pulls me with him

So I do not sediment

In one place.

He is so good

At noticing.

36

Ah.

It is working.

People...are noticing.

They smell the sweet roses crowd the air.

They feel the slosh of coffee lick their ankles.

They hear the crunch of dirt beneath their soles.

And the drip and the scraping.

They see me coming now when I come,

And they begin to whisper.

I wonder if they are nervous.

37

Time for dinner.

Black and Blue people come and join.

They are noticing.

They ask me questions questions questions

And I smile with

Dirt in my white rose teeth.

I am oh so good.

In fact, they say

They will come again.

38

Too bad. Too bad.

I find the Black and Blue

Wrapped tight in petals

And under dirt.

Bee stings can be fatal, they say.

I give them gifts: tears for a song

Left on gold badges before there is dirt.

Too bad. Too bad.

39

My favorite spot for coffee in the afternoon.

Sigh.

It is submerged now

In brown.

Right up to the windows.

The sky is watching.

My shadow spins

For me to go in.

But I just had a swim

And am quite full.

40

No more sleeps. Not ever.

I am at the beach,

In the forest,

Among the clouds.

I am tired now

Of the heavy shadow.

But I am being noticed.

I am noticed.

He is noticing.

The boy.

The boy.

Clouds of petals.

Forests of dirt.

Sands of salt and pepper.

Waves of brown.

Bees kissing me to sleep.

41

We decide to stay.

Perhaps we will be found out.

But until then,

We make a house of shovels.

We pack the cracks with pages and pages.

Tears are so useful,

If only people knew how.

What a lovely cottage.

And we close the lid.

A reluctant click.

42

I make a pile

Of all the things.

Right out in the open

Of my space.

He offers to kiss me.

The boy.

Yes. Yes.

43

How salty sweet.

He has someone to bury.

I cannot see the moon

In our space.

Just black lines as it shines

Through the shovel ceiling.

I wonder if I am nervous.

44

He digs

A hole in my pocket

For me to lie down.

45

I notice

nothing.

46

I notice…

47

No one explains

How hard it is

To get up

Once you lie down

All the way.

Once the dirt is over your face

And the coffee has been poured

And the flowers have been laid.

When you are sediment

And nothing

And then you must be

Movement

And something.

It is too hard.

I am nervous.

I get up.

48

The sky notices.

Tears from the moon.

Whispers like thunder.

Light like cracks.

Drip. Drop.

I slosh in the puddles.

Sometimes,

Spaco stops

When you make room

For a time.

49

I take the long way home.

My shadow scrapes and begs,

But I take the long way home.

In the rain. In the dark. Under the moon.

I hope he is nervous.

50

I am in time for dinner.

51

Confident click. Scooting into my space.

I put the book to my forehead.

Tears have a way of ruining things.

Tears have a way of saving things.

52

I notice,

A drip drop

On the top of my head.

From above?

From above.

I touch the coffee.

It is not.

It is salt and popper water.

Tears.

From above? From above.

53

The boy.

The boy.

I notice him.

He presses his forehead to me.

The tears warp the paper

And make music on the sheet of me.

He breaks the rules.

Takes a pen

To write the end.

No. No.

Books are not for lines!

Books are not for lies!

I try to tell him.

To tell him he is being noticed.

But I am only whispers

And the hum of bees is

Overwhelming.

54

He must be nervous.

I try to stretch across the room,

To open the blinds

So he can see the moon

And how it is changing.

It is changing!

But I cannot reach.

My heels are clamped to his

And he is curled in his space.

I scrape and scrape

To reach.

But I am too heavy.

55

He is at his favorite shop.

He is waiting at a round table,

The sharp edges press into his elbows.

I stare at him from across the room.

I hope he can see the sky peeling back.

From above? From above.

Sometimes. Sometimes.

56

I sit down across from him.

I notice.

I want to touch him.

I want to tell him.

But I only whisper and slosh.

Sometimes...

Whispering is not enough.

Touching is not enough.

Noticing is not enough.

If you cannot reach...

57

He chews the coffee cup.

Bits of ceramic in his perfect teeth.

He swallows and exhales.

Swallows and exhales.

He has made it so much harder.

No one notices.

I want to tell him, but

I am only singing.

Atonal.

Arhythmic.

58

I try to be with him.

I become only his shadow.

I follow him, pull him back,

Scraping and scraping the concrete,

Asphalt under my fingernails.

He thinks I am heavy.

He tries to pry me off.

Bolt cutters. Razors. Tears.

59

I am with him

When it is time for dinner.

There is screaming

From the people who

Must love him

And don't know how.

There is throwing

Of glass.

He puts the shards on his plate

For eating.

I try to whisper,

But it only drips down his neck.

I am noticing!

I am noticing.

60

I take our shovel
To the dirt.
I want to show him
Where once I lay buried—
Drowned in coffee,
Wrapped in petals,
Lulled by bees.
He thinks I am telling him
To lie down,
To fold his hands like pages across his chest.
The boy. The boy.
He is nervous.
Changing is hard.
And losing the sleeps is breaking him.
And dinner is all the time time time.
And no one notices.
No one notices.
No one notices.
But the moon
Does not
Give
up.

More Works by Teshelle Combs

Let There Be Nine Series
- *Let There Be Nine Vol 1:* **Enneagram Poetry**
- *Let There Be Nine Vol 2:* **Enneagram Poetry**

For Series: Words laced together on behalf of an idea, a place, a world.

- **For Her**
- **For Him**
- **For Them**
- **For Us**

Love Bad Series: Poems About Love. Not Love Poems.

- **Love Bad**
- **Love Bad More**
- **Love Bad Best**

Standalone Poetry Books:

Breath Like Glass

Poems for love that never lasts.

Girl Poet

A collection of poems on the passion, privilege, and pain of being (or not quite being) a girl.

FRAMELESS

A collection of poems for the colors that make life vibrant, from their perspective, so we may share in what they might think and feel.

Core Series

Ava is the kind of girl who knows what's real and what isn't. Nothing in life is fair. Nothing is given freely. Nothing is painless. Every foster kid can attest to those truths, and Ava lives them every day. But when she meets a family of dragon shifters and is chosen to join them as a rider, her very notion of reality is shaken. She doesn't believe she can let her guard down. She doesn't think she can let them in—especially not the reckless, kind-eyed Cale. To say yes to him means he would be hers—her dragon and her companion—for life. But what if Ava has no life left to give?

The System Series

1 + 1 = Dead. That's the only math that adds up when you're in the System. Everywhere Nick turns, he's surrounded by the inevitability of his own demise at the hands of the people who stole his life from him. That is, until those hands deliver the bleeding, feisty, eye-rolling Nessa Parker. Tasked with keeping his new partner alive, Nick must face all the ways he's died and all the things he's forgotten.

Nessa might as well give up. The moment she gets into that car, the moment she lays her hazel eyes on her new partner, her end begins. It doesn't matter that Nick Masters can slip through time by computing mathematical algorithms in his mind. It doesn't matter how dark and handsome and irresistibly cold he is. Nessa has to defeat her own shadows. Together and alone, Nick and Nessa make sense of their senseless fates and fight for the courage to change it all. Even if it means the System wins and they end up...well...dead.

Contact Teshelle Combs

Instagram @TeshelleCombs

Email: teshellecombs@gmail.com

Acknowledgments

Thank you to Toni Morrison, who taught me what magical realism can do when we stop thinking in straight lines and square boxes and just write the story the way it comes to us. And thank you to my mom, who didn't call the cops when she read my weird poems and short stories. Also, thank you to teachers and professors, who treasure madness when it's done well.